RUBEN

GRANDPA JACOB'S
FIRST CHRISTMAS DONKEY

Author - E. A. LaPalme

Illustrator - Anne Côté

FOOT NOTES

1. It is recorded that Joachim had passed away some time before Jesus' birth. Here Joachim is alive to help the children identify with Jesus' maternal and paternal grandparents.

2. There may exist some queries about the name Timnah.

Printed in Canada

www.rubenseries.com

Library and Archives Canada Cataloguing in Publication

LaPalme, E. A., 1934-
        Ruben : Grandpa Jacob's first Christmas donkey / E.A. LaPalme ; Anne Cote, illustrator.

ISBN 0-9687215-0-8

        I. Cote, Anne, 1963- II. Title.

PS8623.A72R82 2004   C813'.6   C2004-904521-0

Acknowledgements

Ever since that Christmas Day, nineteen years ago, when the seed for this book was planted, I came in contact with many people that have, in some way, contributed to the realization of "Ruben". Your input is greatly appreciated.

Thank you to the team at Novalis Publishers for your help in the early stages of this project.

The author wishes to thank the following peer reviewers for their contributions during the development of this book:

Father Michael Prieur, Teacher / Author,
St. Peter's Seminary, London, Ontario

Leroy Gorman, Teacher / Author,
Napanee, Ontario

Susan Dignan, English Department Head,
Assumption College, Brantford, Ontario

Jim and Sheila McDermott, Principal, Teacher,
Keswick, Ontario

Gabriel and Joyce Gagnon, Teachers,
Belle River, Ontario

The teachers and students of the Brant and Norfolk Counties who took part in the pilot field-test of "Ruben".

Special Thanks from "Papa"

Thank you to my wife Shirley, my daughters Debbie, Judy and Peggy, my three sons-in-love, Jose, Michael and Richard and to my most precious gift, my seven darling grandchildren, for your enduring love and encouragement. Papa is a very lucky guy!

Ruben, the donkey, was grazing in the olive grove when his grandchildren trotted up to him. Melita, Janna, Kenan, David, Medan, Ben and Benjamin were full of questions.

"Is it true, Zada," as they lovingly called their grandfather, "that you were in the stable in Bethlehem with Mary and Joseph the night Jesus was born?" asked Melita, the eldest.

A warm twinkle appeared in his dark brown eyes.

"Go and get your friends and I'll tell you the story," he said with a smile. Ruben had never seen young donkeys run so fast. Clouds of desert dust swirled around their quickly disappearing hooves.

Within minutes they were back with their friends. The young donkeys crowded around Ruben as he began the story...

Long, long ago, when I was a young donkey, my family and I lived with Joseph's parents, Jacob and Timnah. Once Jesus was born, Joseph's parents became known as Grandpa Jacob and Grandma Timnah.

Joseph and his wife, Mary, lived nearby.

One night, when I was about your age, Grandpa Jacob and Grandma Timnah came to see us in the olive grove.

In a serious voice Grandpa Jacob said, "Mary and Joseph have to go to Bethlehem to be counted. They will need a young donkey with a very strong back to carry their heavy baggage."

Grandma Timnah added, "Jacob, Mary's baby will soon be born. She will have to ride when she is too tired to walk."

Grandpa Jacob looked at my two brothers, Isaac and Esau.

Isaac was very strong, but very stubborn. He did things his way.

Grandpa Jacob shook his head. He needed a donkey that would listen to Joseph and obey.

Esau was also strong but a bit lazy. He would rather play than work. Again, Grandpa Jacob shook his head. He needed a donkey that would work hard on the long journey.

Finally, their heads turned towards me.

"Did you want to go, Zada?" asked young Benjamin.

Yes, I really wanted to go. I stood tall and straight, **praying** that Grandpa Jacob would choose me.

Grandma Timnah whispered, "Ruben is strong, gentle and kind. Perhaps he is the one."

Grandpa Jacob exclaimed, "But he is so young! He has never been away from home before. Timnah, I think that Joseph should come and choose his own donkey."

Later that day, Joseph and his father came to the olive grove. The moment Joseph looked at the **star** on my forehead, he smiled. Pointing at the star, he said, "Father, **Ruben** is the donkey for me." My heart leaped with joy!

Nodding his head, Grandpa Jacob added, "Ruben, now I know why God has placed that **white star** on your forehead. You are **the chosen one!** Your **star** will guide them safely on their journey."

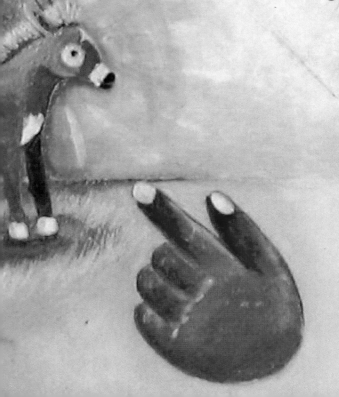

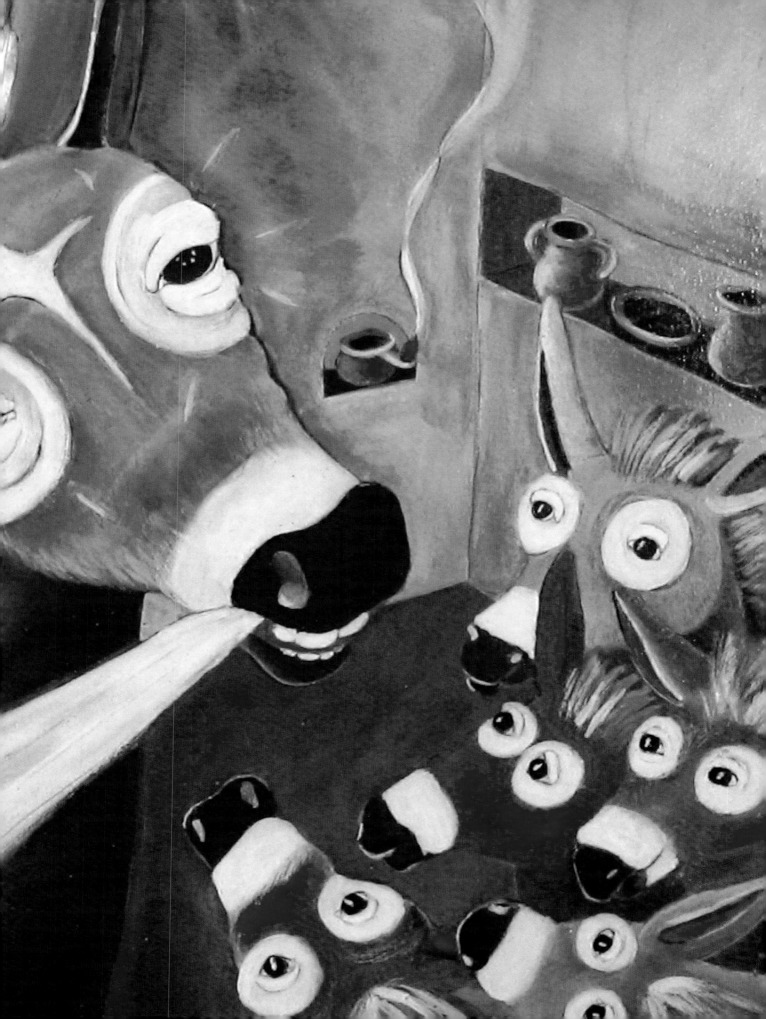

Early the next morning, Grandpa Jacob washed and brushed my coat. He then helped Joseph load the heavy baggage on my back. Shortly after, Joseph said goodbye to his parents and we left to join Mary. She had spent the night visiting with her parents, Ann and Joachim. Because they were Mary's parents they became Grandma Ann and Grandpa Joachim, once Jesus was born.

"Zada, every time we leave on a trip you always lead us in a prayer," pious David said.

"Did you say a prayer before leaving on that special journey to Bethlehem?"

"Yes, my dear David. Grandma Ann and Grandpa Joachim both recited their favourite prayer."
> *"Blessed be the Lord God, the God of Israel,*
> *Who alone works wonders.*
> *May He sweep your path of danger."*

Later that day, we joined a caravan that was also going to Bethlehem. The road was so bumpy that Mary had to ride on my back most of the time. Although I was very careful, she soon became very tired. We had to stop quite often so that she could rest. Some of the people in the caravan became impatient. Joseph did not want to upset them and told the caravan master to go on ahead.

The next day, they left us behind.

Joseph looked after us well on the journey.

We stopped early each evening to find a warm shelter for the night.
He would quickly unpack the heavy baggage from my back and brush
the desert dust from my coat.

While Mary prepared our evening meal, Joseph and I would go and
find wood for the fire.

After sharing some treats, Ben said, "While you were gone to Bethlehem, Zada, Jesus' grandparents must have been lonely."

They missed Mary and Joseph, but they were busy getting things ready for their grandson.

Grandpa Jacob built a beautiful cradle for Jesus.

Grandpa Joachim made some wooden toys for Jesus to play with.

Grandma Timnah wove blankets and sheets for the cradle.

Grandma Ann sewed clothes for Jesus to wear.

We finally reached Bethlehem. The city was crowded with people who had come to be counted.

The time had come for Mary to have her baby.

Most people had arrived in Bethlehem before us, and there were no rooms left in the inns. A kind innkeeper told Joseph that we could stay in his stable.

Joseph spread clean straw in a manger and covered it with one of Grandma Timnah's clean blankets for Mary to lie on.

I became friends with an ox named Rufus who lived there. It was so cold in the stable that Rufus and I stayed close to the manger to keep Mary warm. I was so tired that I fell asleep right away.

A loud snort woke me up with a jolt. "Rufus! What's going on?" I asked.

"Look, Ruben!" said Rufus in amazement. Joseph was holding the most beautiful baby I have ever seen.

"His name is Jesus," he whispered in a trembling voice. "You two will be great friends, Ruben. You will take him wherever he needs to go."

Without wasting any time, Joseph dressed Baby Jesus in swaddling clothes and wrapped him in a warm blanket. He kissed his forehead and gently placed him in his mother's arms.

Ruben closed his huge brown eyes and began shaking his head as big tears started to roll down his long face.

"Why are you crying, Zada?" Medan asked as she hugged him tenderly. Soon all the children's eyes were filled with tears.

I'm sorry, my dear children. For a moment it felt like I was really back in the stable in Bethlehem.Can you believe it? **Jesus**, *born in a* **stable**!

"What about the star, Zada?" asked Kenan.

Rufus and I were so excited at seeing Jesus that we could not sleep. So, we went outside for a walk. "Rufus!" I hollered. *"Look at the big star on top of the stable."*

"Was it bigger than the star on your forehead, Zada?" Janna blurted out.

Oh many, many times bigger! It's still the **biggest star** *I have ever seen.*

As we stood staring at the star, some shepherds arrived.
They had come to see Baby Jesus in the manger.
One of them carried a beautiful baby lamb as a gift.

A few days later, as Rufus and I were standing in the stable yard,
we heard the snort of camels approaching. Three kings who lived
far, far away had followed the **star** for many days to find *Jesus,* the
newborn king. They knelt before *him* and gave *him* presents of gold,
frankincense, and myrrh.

In the middle of that night, I woke up. A bright light was shining right in my eyes. I was young then and very brave, but I could not stop my legs from trembling. As soon as I knew I wasn't dreaming, I nudged Joseph to wake him up.

"What is it, Ruben?" asked Joseph, rubbing his eyes. Seeing an angel, Joseph softly murmured, "Who are you?"

"Do not be afraid," the angel said. "God has sent me to bring you a message. King Herod wants to harm Baby Jesus. You must go to Egypt. You must leave at once!"

Mary heard the angel's words and was very worried. "Joseph, if we leave now, Jesus' grandparents won't even know that Jesus is born. What are we going to do?"

"Mary, some of our friends are going back to Nazareth tomorrow," Joseph said, trying to comfort her. "I am sure that they will tell our parents about their grandson and explain why we must flee to Egypt."

Time passed.

Back home in Nazareth, Grandma Ann had rocked Jesus' empty cradle for over a year.
She had hummed her favourite lullaby over and over again.
Oh, how his grandparents wished they could see him!
Egypt was so far away and Mary and Joseph had been gone for **so long**!

Many more months went by.

One day, Grandpa Joachim and Grandma Ann hurried over to visit Grandpa Jacob and Grandma Timnah.

"We just heard that King Herod is dead,"
Grandpa Joachim told them.

"This means that Mary and Joseph can return home!" exclaimed Grandma Timnah.

"Ann, our prayers are answered! Our *grandson*, **Jesus**, will soon be here!"

"The cradle I made will be too small for him now," said Grandpa Jacob. "Jesus will soon be three years old! Tomorrow I will start making my grandson a bigger bed."

"Oh!" said Grandma Ann. "The baby clothes I made will never fit im now! I have to get busy sewing again."

he days flew by as Jesus' grandparents busily prepared for him to me home.
heir hearts were overflowing with love and joy.
hey couldn't wait to see him!

We arrived back home in Nazareth on Jesus' third birthday, Christmas Day. His grandparents had a big party to welcome us. Lots of family and friends came to celebrate. There was a big feast and music and presents.

Overcome with joy and happiness, Jesus' grandparents praised and thanked the Lord for their **gift**. After waiting three long years, they were finally able to hug and kiss their grandson, Jesus, for the very first time.

I was so happy to see my family again after being away for so long.
I had grown so much; they hardly recognized me.

"Who is the young boy holding on to your tail, Ruben?" Mother asked.

I told her that he was my best friend, Jesus, the son of Mary and
Joseph, who was born on Christmas Day in a manger in Bethlehem.

The author is seen above sharing the first proof of his book with his seven grandchildren. Seated beside "Papa" are Megan and Dylan. Standing from left to right are: Brent, Jenna, Kevin, Melanie and Blaine.

February 6, 1985, was a day of great happiness for me. My first grandchild, Melanie, was born. I will always cherish my first Christmas as a grandfather. However, I still cannot explain the feeling of nostalgia that came over me when her parents took her to see Baby Jesus in Grandma's manger. There was no grandfather in the manger! This caused me to ponder for many years why Jesus' grandparents had been omitted in the First Christmas story. I wrote "Ruben" so that the children can identify more closely with Jesus, the Christ Child, by realizing that he too had loving grandparents. I am sure that they cherished their grandchild as much as I cherish my own grandchildren.

E. A. LaPalme

The Illustrator, Anne Côté:
Born in Montreal in 1963, Anne has earned a Bachelor's Degree in Graphic Design and conceptual Arts plus a Bachelor's Degree in Plastic Arts from the University of Quebec located in Montreal and Hull, Quebec. Many Advertising Agencies and Publishers have benefited from Anne's gift as an Illustrator and Graphic Designer. She has taught Graphic Design and Illustration in Canada and South America.

Presently, Anne works as a Freelance Illustrator and Graphic Designer.

Watch for other upcoming titles in the "Ruben" series.